Earthquake Weather

Volume 33
Sun Tracks An American Indian Literary Series

Series Editor
Ofelia Zepeda

Editorial Committee
Vine Deloria, Jr.
Larry Evers
Joy Harjo
N. Scott Momaday
Emory Sekaquaptewa
Leslie Marmon Silko

Janice Gould

Earthquake Weather

Poems

The University of Arizona Press
Tucson

For Marie-Elise

I would like to thank the Astraea Foundation for a grant enabling the completion of this volume—J. G.

Several of the poems in this collection have appeared, some in a slightly different form, in the following publications: *American Poetry Review; Berkeley Poetry Review; Blue Mesa Review; Frontiers; Hembra; Callaloo; Outlook; The Poetry of Sex,* edited by Tee Corinne; *Returning the Gift,* edited by Joseph Bruchac (University of Arizona Press, 1994); and *The Sound of Rattles and Clappers,* edited by Greg Sarris (University of Arizona Press, 1994).

The University of Arizona Press
© 1996 by Janice Gould
All rights reserved

01 00 99 98 97 96   6 5 4 3 2 1

Library of Congress Cataloging-in-Publication Data
Gould, Janice, 1949–
Earthquake weather : poems / Janice Gould.
p.   cm. — (Sun tracks ; v. 33)
ISBN 0-8165-1610-3 (cloth : alk. paper). — ISBN 0-8165-1630-8
(paper : alk. paper)
1. Indians of North America—California—Poetry. 2. Indians—
Mixed descent—Poetry.   I. Title.   II. Series.
PS501.S85   vol. 33
[PS3557.0862]
810.8 s—dc20
[811'.54]   95-32544

British Cataloguing-in-Publication Data
A catalogue record for this book is available from the British Library.

Contents

Preface

When I was nine years old, my father lost his job at a U.S. Navy laboratory in San Diego, California, and my family moved north to Berkeley to live with my mother's adopted mother. The move enabled my father to return to school to earn another university degree; this proved a good step, and led eventually to his finding another way to support his family.

The move to Berkeley could be summarized in a number of ways. For me, it meant leaving a small, two-bedroom tract home in a Point Loma neighborhood full of baby boomers, and moving into the considerably older neighborhood and more spacious house that my adopted grandmother, Beatrice Lane, had built in the 1920s. Our house, one of the old ones in the Berkeley Hills, was on a steep, narrow street not far from the crest of the hills. It was white stucco, had a tile roof, and was semi-surrounded by redwood trees. The large front garden was overgrown with box hedges, various shrubs and trees, ferns, and an assortment of flowers—trillium, calla lilies, day lilies, sweet william—that did well enough in acidic soil and abundant shade. Our neighborhood in San Diego carried the smell of pungent succulents and the chaparral that grew in the sandy cliffs along Point Loma; our neighborhood in Berkeley smelled of blue-gum eucalyptus and damp, loamy soil. Those notorious thick fogs blew in during the summer months, making the house chilly enough to warrant using the fireplace and wearing wool sweaters all day long.

My two sisters and I spent a lot of time roaming the hills on foot and on bicycle, peddling our way to the top of Grizzly Peak Road, then zooming down at top speed, pretending to set world records. On our excursions onto the University of California property, a ten-minute walk from our house, we were careful to avoid poison oak in the dry, shrubby ravines, and milkweed and thistles in the grassy hills. We had to be wary of rattlesnakes, skunks, and porcupines, too. More than once we had to bathe a dog in tomato juice or delicately pull quills from a sore and swollen nose.

It was at my adopted grandmother's house where I became most firmly attached and sensitive to my California Indian—that is, Koyangk'auwi (or Konkow) Maidu—heritage.[1] Perhaps it was because of Berkeley's proximity to the Sierra Nevada and the small town of Belden, on the Feather River, where my mother, Vivian Beatty, was born in 1914. Beatrice had photographs of that region on her walls, mementos of places she and her two sisters had stayed while on their many trips into the Sierra Nevada. The hand-tinted photos of the Feather River in Plumas County, and of Belden, were particularly interesting to me. My mother's father, Harry Beatty Sr., had homesteaded property about a mile west of Belden, on a rivulet named Little Indian Creek. My mother, the youngest of fourteen children born to Harry and Helen (Nellie) Beatty, lived there until she was four or five years old. That was when Nellie died of cancer and my mother was adopted by the Lane sisters: Beatrice, Henrietta, and Clara.

The Lane sisters had long been interested in adopting an Indian child. They liked my mother, Vivian, who was bright and sweet. My mother knew how to read at the age of three or four, and had a precocious vocabulary, gathered from older

1. There are variant spellings of the word "Konkow": Concow, Konkau, and Konkow, all anglicizations of the word "koyangk'auwi," meaning "meadowland," the name the "Konkow" gave themselves. The Maidu language has three divisions: Maidu, Konkow, and Nisenan. The Maidu people lived in the high meadows of the Sierra Nevada and along the watersheds of several northern Sierra Nevada rivers that generally flow in a southwestern direction. These include the Feather, the Yuba, the Bear, the American, and the Cosumnes Rivers. Before the Native people had contact with Europeans, Maiduan languages were spoken in a territory bordered on the north by Chico Creek and including the confluences of Deer Creek and Mill Creek where they meet the Sacramento River. This northern border extended northeast past Mount Lassen and beyond the Susan River. Thus the eastern border fell east of the Sierra Nevada crest. The Cosumnes River formed the southern boundary, and to the west, Maidu speakers lived along Butte Creek and the Sacramento River.

siblings, adults, and whomever she met. Apparently the Lane sisters and my mother's parents had arranged for them to take Vivian when they learned Nellie would not survive her illness. I do not know if there was ever a legal adoption.

The Lane sisters' interest in Indians may have been piqued during their childhood in the state of Kansas. They came from a family of liberal-minded Episcopalians. The sisters had moved together to the San Francisco Bay area just before the famous earthquake of 1906. Many of their belongings were stored in warehouses that went up in flames as fires spread throughout San Francisco. When we visited Berkeley, before we moved in with Beatrice, we ate our cereal out of ceramic bowls patched and glued together, with brown, resinous seams—survivors from the wreckage of that earthquake.

I first saw the country where my mother was born, and to which she returned frequently after her mother's death, the year before we moved to Berkeley. Returning from a short stay in northern Idaho, we drove down Highway 395, turned west at Susanville, and drove along the shores of Lake Almanor, past Greenville, and down the north fork of the Feather River. I remember that the day was rainy, that low clouds drifted over the mountainous ridges above the river canyon as we approached Belden. Waterfalls tumbled down the shale and granite slopes, and creeks spilled through steep canyons flanked with oak, cedar, pine, and dogwood. Abundant springs were seeping up from underground, fissuring their way through rock, including a spring of soda water near what had been the Beatty homestead. This homestead, it seems, had been sold to, or somehow acquired by, the Pacific Gas and Electric Company, which had installed hydroelectric dams on the Feather River up as far as Rich Bar. The PG&E leased the acquired homestead land to various enterprises: a resort with a gas pump, a tiny café.

We stopped at the confluence of Yellow Creek and the Feather River where the highway crossed the creek and the road widened. My mom showed us the trail that led up to a small cemetery where most of her immediate family lay buried. The last time my mother had been there, I think, was probably in January of 1946, the year her father died. It was a nineteenth-century cemetery, the sort you find all over the Mother Lode country. In it we spied pieces of an old-fashioned, cast-iron fence still standing, and on crumbling notecards, the fading names of my mother's family: her father, some brothers and sisters, perhaps a cousin or two. Her mother and grandmother had been buried on the homestead property.

We visited the canyon many times as we were growing up. One of my aunties, Lillian, had moved back to Belden with her husband, Ivan Brockett. For years they leased a one-room stone-sided cabin up the river. Right outside their front door was a fresh-water spring that they tapped for drinking water; and beyond the green lawn outside their back door, my uncle planted in the fertile river soil one of his huge gardens full of sunflowers, vegetables, and strawberries.

Another of my mother's siblings, a brother, Ernest, lived in Quincy with his wife, Hazel, probably an Achumawi, and her two boys from an earlier marriage, Beuford and Charles. Ernest worked in one of the lumber mills. When we visited these relatives, it was for brief summer vacations away from Berkeley, a week here, a weekend there. We kids went hiking, or to the swimming hole on the river, or we went fishing with one of my uncles. We spent time driving around the dirt logging roads north of the canyon, up around Butt Lake and Humbug Valley. In this way, we became acquainted with some of the country where our Indian ancestors had lived for thousands of years.

That country was a source of deep pleasure for me, but also a source of sadness and loss. Though my connection to that land was intense, full of love and curiosity, there was a limit to how much I could know from a familial or "tribal" source. So many of my relatives had died. Both of my mother's parents were long underground before I came along, as were many of my aunts and uncles. Nellie's death caused a huge disruption in my mother's family. Harry Beatty Sr. seems to have gone to pieces, more or less abandoning his family. My mother's siblings dispersed, finding jobs wherever they could. When my sisters and I were growing up, we had little knowledge of surviving family members, and hardly knew of their existence.

What we do know of the Beattys, Harry's family, and the Osiers (or Ociers), Nellie's family, goes back only about three generations. Our maternal great-grandfather, Jacques Osier, married a Konkow woman who lived in Yankee Hill. My mother told me that Osier was a Frenchman who worked as an engineer overseeing the building of the Southern Pacific Railroad through the Feather River canyon. He and his wife moved to Belden, where my grandmother, Helen, was born. Harry's father was Thomas Beatty, an Irishman, and one of the first miners on the Feather River. He and his wife, Mary, also a Konkow, apparently had a homestead near Belden. Mary's father was the notorious old medicine man from Berry Creek named Dr. Charley. His wife was Emma Charley.

In spite of the disruption and dislocation of the family, Harry Beatty Sr. had the foresight to enroll himself and his kids on the Concow tribal enrollment with the federal government sometime in the 1920s. The tribal rolls were closed, I believe, around 1950, after I was born.

The displacement and dissolution of my Indian family represents one aspect of the colonization that took place in northern California. This colonization amounted, in many ways, to a social and political upheaval that occurred at the level of community and, perhaps more crucially, within families. In California, the losses of Indian land and life were enormous and rapid, particularly after 1850. The outright murder of Native people was serious enough, but add to that the decimation of populations through disease, warfare, and starvation, through periods of removal and relocation, through assimilative state and federal policies, and one can begin to understand how difficult it is to piece together a family from shards of memory and fragments of cultural knowledge.

As a mixedblood of European and Koyangk'auwi descent, I have sought answers to questions about my identity. Although I am enrolled as a Concow Maidu, I am uncertain what that means. Since racism was pervasive in my family, on both sides, I learned from my Anglo grandparents that to be "mixedblood" was cause for shame and concern: my skin would always be "dark" to their way of seeing, I would never be as white as they were. The "taint" of being Indian meant that I might eventually fall into "degenerate" ways. It was clear to some in the family that what might save me from being a low-class savage was my "European blood."

In the face of such hostility, disguised as concern and good intentions, my mother remained proud of her Indian "blood," and proud of her children. Being on the defensive, she learned to "pass" as the respectable, bourgeois woman she was. On the other hand, she capitalized from time to time on her Indian appearance, if that proved useful. She grew up in a period of intense assimilation, perhaps particularly if one was a "half-breed" in California. Her individual circumstances certainly warranted an effort to fit in, to not be different, and to relegate her Indianness to the past, if that were possible. Nevertheless, Mama taught us kids that we were Konkow Indians, and she was emphatic that we should not be ashamed of this. She could not provide us, however, with a cultural heritage, which had been unraveling in our family for at least two generations as a consequence of intermarriage and the colonial legacy. Understanding our cultural heritage was something we had to do for ourselves: studying the hidden (and overt) "otherness" of our own lives, and tracing our family's being through ethnographic accounts, linguistic data, local histories, folklore, and whatever had not passed out of our relatives' memories.

I came to writing many years ago, in part as a way to record what it means for me to be a Koyangk'auwi mixedblood. I offer the poetry in this volume as a sort of testimony from a member of a disrupted Indian family. These poems could be likened to those fields of wildflowers that bloom in what are left of open places all over a state that is never far from my state of heart or mind.

Plays on the "white guilt" or how whites romanticized Natives - could be advantageous to be Indian.

Acknowledgments

I wish to express my gratitude to the following friends and family for their love, support, and encouragement: Janet Adelman, Paula Gunn Allen, Judith Barrington and Ruth Gundle, Barbara Bentley, Chrystos, Nancy Gage, Tess Gallagher, Minrose Gwin and Ruth Salvaggio, Joy Harjo, Robert Hass, Terrell and Jennifer Johnson, Louis Owens, Christian McEwen, Barb McGuire, Wanda Martin, Catherine Michaelis, Deborah Miranda, Jean Molesky, Lauren Muller, John Randall, Margaret Randall and Barb Byers, Ann Rasmussen, Greg Sarris, Sue Schweik, Vickie Sears, Dan and Marilyn Smith, Patricia Clark Smith, Winifred Steiner, Mary Beth Train, Hertha Wong, and Carolyn Woodward. Thanks also to editors at the University of Arizona Press, particularly Ofelia Zepeda and Joanne O'Hare. Thanks especially to my soul-partner, Mimi Wheatwind.

This Energy in Which We Exist

Mornings Are Like This

Each morning I wake with the sun
wanting to know how the day will begin.

I go to the kitchen
with its cracked floor and blue walls
and make coffee, feed the cats.

If it is summer,
                I open doors
and windows,
and look out on the world—
the cottonwood,
           the fence,
                      a south wind
with its promise of rain.

A few blocks away
           a train passes.
Two houses down
           someone starts his pickup.

That's my world.

I want to know
           the secrets of this life,
break them
           in a thousand pieces.

I will seize the cold fragments,
and hold them fiercely
           to the morning light.

3

Ants

This morning I am running by the ditch.
Already the day is warm and humid.
To my left are fields of alfalfa and corn,
the horse pastures of the rich.
Rows of cottonwoods, high-crowned and full,
border the fields. Beyond the trees
the river twists and shimmers.

Earlier I had passed workmen
thinning the undergrowth with chainsaws.
When I saw them I began to walk,
averting my face slightly.
I know I am an ugly woman.
I didn't want to see them talk behind their hands
or jeer out loud at me.

After passing them, I ran. Sometimes
the soil along the ditch is soft,
kicked up by rabbits, dogs, and large toads
who park themselves beneath the deadly nightshade.
In other places the earth is hard, a pale pink.

Ants are busy on this trail,
black *hormigas* and red ones,
such sturdy fellows!
I pass one struggling with a two-inch twig.
Here is another bearing a bird's small feather.
How selfless they seem. How strong.
Beneath the surface of the road
they've built cities of amber,
cities of gold, cities of obsidian.
Subterranean tunnels must run for miles
connecting colony after colony,
beneath the fields,
beneath the river.
Under the domes of the volcanos
exist vast chambers
full of music, the sound of rock
being chiselled by a million workers.

I like how the ants are busy
and oblivious. They work every shift
with such purpose: building, repairing,
making something beautiful for their own eyes.

We can never see how they live, how they dream
their sweet and crystalline existences,
tunneling deeper and deeper into earth.

Sunday Mornings

You love Sunday mornings though they make you melancholy. They say Sunday is the first day of our week, but that isn't true. It is the last day of the old week, the day you say farewell to the brief weekend freedom you have known.

That is why it is best to rise early on a Sunday. Sipping your coffee, you turn on the radio. The melodies of Albéniz or de Falla spill out, virtuous music. Even if the morning is cold, the clouds dark and misty, the warmth of music causes Spanish mountains to appear, dry and pine covered. The sky is blue, a breeze stirs the needles of the trees. In the distance, the ocean. A hawk drifts overhead on a current of air.

Or it may be that rain starts suddenly to fall on a city outside your window, a place you have seen only in dreams. A pedestrian walks by on the cobbled street, her hair covered by lace: she is on her way to Mass. In the narthex of the church she lights two candles, one for the brother who perished in combat, one for the daughter who died from cancer. She sits in her usual pew, the prayerbook unopened in her lap. The crucified body hangs nearby, suggesting this is the bloodiest day of the week.

Or if you have not risen early, if you have slept late and soundly, you will devote the afternoon to browsing in bookstores. You will meet a friend in a café, a woman you love and with whom you want to spend more time. Chatting over latte, she might guilelessly reveal to you the things that shaped her strangeness: an ability to leave her body and fly around the earth; an ability to cause the rain to fall or cease; an ability to always know which direction is north. You smile and listen, but you are aware, as she talks, that the workweek comes quickly, that tomorrow you must face the office, the printshop, or school. You wish Sunday could extend infinitely—like wings moving across the distant watery horizon, well on past the meridians and datelines of the world.

Blood Sisters

For Deborah

I did not know how lonely I was
till we began to talk.
You told me of the Mission,
the Book of Names,
and the photos you discovered.
Each offered a remote clue
about your family,
Chumash ancestors,
things you thought permanently lost.
I told you about the Maidu song my mother sang
in a scale I could never learn,
and about the tree on an old dirt road
where the white men lynched my people.

In our separate childhoods, we each
read that Indians were stupid,
lived like swine or dogs.
Such ignorant lies!
The Chumash were flogged and tortured,
the Maidu stolen for slaves,
and later marched at gunpoint
to a distant reservation.

We glance at one another,
fall silent.
Americans do not know these things
nor do they want to know.

But each of us knows stories
we have never even whispered.

What Happened to My Anger

What happened to my anger?
It was rounded up
and removed to a camp.
Or it went into self-exile.
Or perhaps it painted itself white.
Now it goes into the world
with a happy face.

What happened to my anger?
It turned into a worm
coiled in my belly.
It formed into a mass of cold cells
attached to my spleen.
It became this wound
in my hand.

What happened to my anger?
It became a eunuch
and laid itself down on the divan
before the flickering TV,
drowning its sorrow
in vacuity.
It went to the kitchen in search of food,
prepared many meals.
It cleaned the toilet,
the catbox,
the carpet.

My anger has not worn itself out.
It has not become obedient,
but dumb.

Evening News

Each evening the news,
unbearable and desperate,
is delivered by a man
with a dispassionate face.
The ads spell relief,
promoting laxatives,
pain pills,
automobiles.

When you turn off the set
there is darkness
and unnatural silence.
Beyond the windows and doors
the city builds itself:
cathedrals, museums,
convenience stores.
By midnight
there is an audible crescendo.
Then the traffic subsides,
sirens die out.

This is when germination
takes place, the secret
unfolding of things.
Those who scavenge come out,
those who commit atrocities.
And ghosts who inhabit
the carcasses of dogs
set up a howl.

In a country bereft of love,
citizens are fearful
and suspicious: they wish
to know the "truth," not
always what is written.
Out among the galaxies
is wild, crazy singing—
the hard fiery mystery of words.

Friday Evening

Friday evening is my favorite one to think about. I like to imagine how on that evening along the northwest coast, fog steals in over the water, the green islands, the streets of the cities. I can see how the country looks, as if I were flying in from some place far away. I look back and see the deep forests and the land to the east, already dark, already giving itself up to night, the vastness of night about which we know so little. Ahead are the lights of the big ports: San Francisco, Portland, Seattle. And between the miles of cloudy glare are miles of darkness and the end of the day, the end of the workweek. Sour-smelling men fall asleep on their sofas, and women sit on the edges of bathtubs, rubbing sore feet. Children who are hungry for their suppers get scrappy and quarrel.

I think how sad this country is: people sit at home watching TV while fog billows its way into their neighborhoods. Behind stucco walls are unknown needs. In closets and bureaus, loneliness is folded among the soft underclothes of families. Perhaps one child has gone off to read. She wears the peculiar look of absorption that haunts the face of one so alone among others. There are things that perplex her, things she can't understand. I know there are doors in her house before which she stands, hesitant. I see her now in the yellow kitchen. She has left her reading to wonder about these doors, to peer down the stairs and open the trap in the basement wall that exposes the dark underside of the house, the maze of pipes and rafters, beams and girders that shore up the geometry of this dwelling.

High above the house the universe spills open, alive in the dark eternal wind. Might the mysterious patterns of stars spell a remote geography? At first glance, the lights of the airplane look like stars—red, blue, a faint green. They twinkle as the plane veers earthward. Below us the tarmac is clear and trees listen with their usual intensity. The earth holds its breath. As we descend through wet fog, windows are spattered with moisture, and then comes the jolt of contact as we hit the runway. The plane speeds whatever direction the pilot takes us before he throws the engines in reverse, and in a sudden decrescendo we slow to what seems an almost human pace. The passengers let out a collective sigh and we begin to gather ourselves together. We can hardly wait to stand, stretch, walk off this plane we're all on. We can hardly wait to enter the brightly lit terminal and find our families, a phone booth, a quick stiff drink before hailing a cab and heading for our long-lost homes.

Outside Language

We are not all that is possible. None of us has ever
really experienced justice. None of us has known
enough tenderness. —June Jordan

For Sue

When my mother's soul
slipped through the brief
disappearing O of her mouth,
I saw her speak the language
they say only newborns
or the dead can speak,
murmured words of greeting
and farewell.
I felt her slip away,
a presence just beyond
my apprehension.

        I wondered why
I couldn't go too,
·because this material world
meant nothing to me. I understood
that things stay together
through our vigilance.
If I let the boundaries
fail for a moment,
I'd begin to fall
past the ground that shores us up,
through the roots of trees,
beds of lava and flint,
clear to the other side
of the universe.

The first morning without my mother
it rained—
that was a sign—
and the world was suddenly with me,
vivid and palpable.
I could feel the weight of history
drag at my feet, but
something poured into me
like music, and I knew
she wanted me to accept
my own fate,
the fulfillment of the life
she gave me.

And I felt the words that came
from the other side of memory and knowledge.
They had less to do with justice
than tenderness,
less to do with love
than courage.

The Day of the Dead

I wish it were like this:
el día de los muertos comes
and we fill our baskets with bread,
apples, chicken, and beer,
and go out to the graveyard.

We bring flowers with significant colors—
yellow, crimson, and gold—
the strong hungry colors of life,
full of saliva and blood.

We sit on the sandy mounds
and I play my accordion.
It groans like the gates of hell.
The flames of the votives
flicker in the wind.

My music makes everything sway,
all the visible and invisible—
friends, candles, ants, the wind.
Because for me life ripens,
and for now it's on my side
though it's true I am often afraid.

I wear my boots when I play the old squeeze-box,
and stomp hard rhythms
till the headstones dance on their graves.

This Energy in Which We Exist

For Joy

Somehow it is true, this energy in which we exist,
like the force of music that streams
into and out of our hearts, the muscle itself
clenching, releasing, converting one thing
into another: anger into hatred, hatred into blood,
blood into love. And none of this easy

to explain, none of this possible in isolation—
though in isolation it happens too—
because we are shaped by a harmony
that is at once terrible
and wonderful, assonant and dissonant,
one moment a masked deity,
the next a water monster
swimming the crest of a wave. One moment
we are smoke, the next fire; now a war,
an infant, a hand,
a kiss, breath, bird,

or sunlight. We are something
that comes from nothing,
nothing from something.
Who knows how long we hoped—each of us—
to enter this world? So much potential
waiting to be fulfilled. Magic is
at the center of things: I was a rabbit
curled at the bottom of a silk hat.
Then something seized me, lifting me
from this envelope. I sloughed off

the skin of that other life. Now
I see how we must decide,
how we must make a choice.
We think we are limited,
but forms are tricky things.
At the level where hearts dissolve,
maps have no meaning.

Anguish and love drive us ceaselessly
from one existence to the next.

Questions about the Soul

I have questions about the soul
who resides like a dark cousin
in the shadow of my heart.

I remember her black curly hair,
the almond shape of her eyes,
and her small mouth
turned down at the edges.

Her voice could not reach her mother.
When she rattled the cage of her crib,
her mother sang louder.

Here in this photo, pudgy and laughing,
she is dressed in a crocheted sweater.
She was a brown, sturdy baby.
But her little boots are dirty.

Where did she live, this soul,
with whom did she take her supper?
Did she sleep in a solitary room?
Did she know her father?

Perhaps her mother had beaten her—
I heard that she ran away.
They say she grew up mean, and took
many unruly lovers.

I have questions about the soul—
how she survived her sorrow,
whether she could love, or if
she hated her sons and daughters.

I have questions about the soul
who resides like history
in my heart's dark chamber.

A Berkeley Life

Alphabet

A is a mountain whose steep ascent
leads to a pinnacle
from which you can view
the extent of these shapes.
B is for flesh,
the letter of home.
C is the first coil of a basket,
and a severed ear.
D is the belly of the moon
or a bear.
E represents three paths
from the main road.
One path leads to an inner place.
F hobbles on one foot,
while G rolls upon the dusty earth.
H shows the banks of a canal
crossed by a narrow bridge
in winter.
I is solitary.
J is a jack to the king's K
who is really a knave.
L is the right angle of pain.
M is a fish
swimming toward heaven,
while N plunges toward darkness.
O opens and illumines the night.
P is proud and pedantic.
Q is a monkey's cage,
his tail the only thing free.
R is a sailor's device,
having to do with sextants
and stars.

S leads to the Milky Way,
or earthbound becomes the vine
that circles a tree.
T stands for the forest
where the most mysterious letters
live in huts and caves.
U sends you back
the way you came.
V is the meteor's descent,
W the neighbor's fence,
while X marks a crossroad
where you decide: Christian
or Pagan?
Y represents choice. Z
is the zigzag
of the path
back home
or away.

Nightfall

How Blue blue appears at dusk
after the sun has set
and cold emerges from who knows where.
The streets empty
and porch lights flick on.
In another time a family
sits down together
for its evening meal:
chicken, dumplings, peas,
and carrots in a thick broth.

The windows in the dining room are steamy.
Later one child,
always the same one,
draws with her index finger
a picture in the condensation:
a man, a house, a tree,
a smiling face that runs
and becomes a frown.

Outside, in the evening light, the pyracantha's
red berries seem suddenly to glow,
tendrils of ivy inch
between the stepping stones.
The earth shifts a bit
easing its hold on various bulbs—
the scallions, the brodiaea,
the wild iris
whose petals remain folded.

Saturday Morning

Saturday morning rain. All night the clouds moved in over the coast, swelling in waves of cold moisture. All night the sea rose, clouds lowered against the hills and the bay rippled in gray-green waves; whitecaps foamed in competing currents of wind and water.

Saturday morning, and rain trickles down the tossing boughs of the redwood tree that scratched the windows all night. Rain spatters against the old glass in the pane—glass that long ago ran and buckled until the windows became distorted. And though the sky is dark and cloudy, it lightens enough to wake the girl who has slept, unaware of the rain. Now she hears it pattering and lets out a long sigh, knowing the weariness the day will bring. After breakfast she will strip the beds and pile the laundry in the entry hall. While her two sisters work upstairs, she will sit on the floor sorting darks, lights, towels, tablecloths, bedding. All morning the basement will steam with washing. In the meantime, someone gets out the brown canister-shaped vacuum, its cloth bag full of dust and hair. One sister vacuums, another makes the beds. Then the girl cleans the bathroom, scrubbing out the sink, toilet, and tub with white scouring powder. Her mother runs a dust mop over the upstairs hall and then sweeps, pushing the broom into the corners where walls join, sweeping hard in lifelong consternation. One sister does the dishes that have piled up, the pans full of cold soapy water. The other sister washes down the stove and counters, cleans the cabinet doors, scrubs away the scum of grease from the top of the refrigerator. Then all three girls dutifully carry their father's shoes upstairs, along with his papers, tools, gadgets, sweater, and their own shoes, books, and jackets.

All the while they have been working, rain has fallen on the tile roof of the house, and the rain troughs, loaded with leaves, overflow in a cold waterfall. Rain settles in the tall trees and in the garden. When her grandmother was alive, the girl quietly entered her dim green room, the room with the hand-tinted photos. She remembers bringing her grandmother a poached egg and toast on a tray, strong tea in a white teapot. Her job was to straighten her grandmother's room while the old woman ate. She dusted the dresser with furniture oil, lining up brush and comb. She arranged the set of ivory-handled manicure tools on a clean dresser cloth, embroidered by the girl's forgotten older half-sister.

Later, the girl sets up the ironing board in the living room while an old movie plays on the black-and-white TV. She stands, watching the movie, ironing the stiff sheets and tablecloths that come out of the laundry, folding each piece so the corners match exactly. If the job is done poorly, her mother makes her do it again. But sometimes, in a fit of exasperation, her mother pushes the daughter aside, shakes out the offending cloth, and begins to iron it herself. She thumps the iron down, pressing so hard the board creaks. The daughter watches, hurt. Her mother's face is creased with its usual fury. She finishes ironing the tablecloth and, not looking at her daughter, carefully takes another cloth out of the wicker laundry basket and opens it out on the board. The girl protests. "I can do it," she tells her mother. But her mother doesn't look at her, just takes up the sprinkling bottle and shakes it over the cloth. The girl watches the water pock the cloth like gray rain.

Outside, the rain has subsided, and a glow from the setting sun illuminates the garden. Everything is wet and dripping: ferns, moss, the leaves of the pyracantha. The walkway of stones is strewn with fallen redwood leaves, over which large yellow slugs make their way, groping and silent.

Trying to Hold On

You are thinking of Berkeley,
the way it was when you were growing up,
before the Free Speech and the anti-war
"demos" on Sproul Plaza.

The wind, bitter or salty,
always blew.
The scent of laurel leaves
in cold canyons
gave you a headache
as you walked home from school.

And those damp meadows
always so muddy: I remember
the goofy way you'd slip and fall,
face-down,
racing with your dogs.

Years of terrible math
were yours,
along with history,
physics,
and English.
The silence you endured
in public schools!
Some things you can't laugh off.

Your breasts grew, hair
appeared on your legs,
your period began late
and haphazardly. Your sweat
acquired a bad odor, pungent
and irreconcilable.
It announced your fear,
the anger that hardened inside you
and sharpened your wicked tongue.

Who were you? What did you want?
Were you a person?

I remember your lowered head,
thick black hair,
and how on the way home
your hands would open
and you would drop your books,
your oboe in its case,
letting them crash on the sidewalk.

You were thinking, "What's wrong with me?
Where do I belong? Why
am I here? Why can't I
hold on?"

The Sixties

1.
When the fire hoses were turned
on the Negro citizens
of those southern towns—
on mourners, protesters,
human beings—
the spray blew men, women,
and children off their feet.
Bodies rolled helplessly
on the pavement,
while the white men who shot them down
laughed. "We'll wash those vermin
down the river and out to sea."
They were pleased with the humiliation.

Miles away in California
I watched on TV,
and tasted a pure hatred.
I was nothing
if not passionate.
But I had to be careful
not to show too much,
or I risked being taunted
by my mother who called me
"nigger-lover."
I remember seeing on her lips
the spittle of contempt.

When the churches were bombed
and protesters beaten,
when the lynched bodies
were cut from trees,
and the men who did the lynching
sat smirking in the knowledge
they would go free,
I tasted pure bile,
the vinegar of muted dissent,
the salt of fugitive tears.
A firestorm of rage
built in me
as I watched my mother
take Communion on Sundays
and afterwards leave the church,
high and mighty,
like the Indian Princess
she imagined herself to be.

2.

When the conflagrations started
in Detroit and Watts,
my mother triumphed.
The towns were in blazes,
the looters shot
through shattered windows
of store-fronts and houses.
The damned "niggers,"
so arrogant and lawless,
were getting what they deserved!
How then could I condone those people
who didn't care about rule or order,
those thieves, rapists,
welfare artists?

Dr. King had been shot,
Medgar Evers, and Malcolm X.
The white men who controlled things
were still in power.
In Viet Nam the war was raging.
Every day I was more frightened
as I felt a riotous resistance
fist in my heart,
the stench of burning tar
and asphalt pour down my throat.
What are you? she'd ask.
A communist?
A lesbian?
A damned subversive?

I endured her hatred,
her contradictions. After church
she wanted to slap me silly
because I was sassy and unrepentant.
I said I wanted justice.

When the flames of antipathy
raced down the hall in our house
and beat on the door of my room,
when even self-laceration
did nothing to stifle those words
so carefully chosen to destroy me,
I would tip down the brandy
and imagine myself lying in a snowy meadow,
winking back at the pure cold points of fire
that greeted me from afar.

Thursdays

They say one should never wear green on Thursday, for fear of being labeled a queer. This we heard when we were young, but it was difficult to determine what a queer was. Was it a man who shunned society, who let his hair grow long and chose to live alone on some mountain? Was it a balding man with horn-rimmed glasses who read philosophy and thought too much? Was a queer the lunatic who berated everyone, who stood in the middle of Shattuck Avenue and shook his fist at amused motorists? Or was it a man whose penchant for taking women's roles in comic operas and singing in falsetto betrayed an inordinate interest in dressing and posing as a woman?

Could a girl be queer? Could a woman? What would such a lady look like, and what would she do? I suspected I was queer. By mistake I sometimes wore a dark green skirt to school on Thursdays, a store-bought plaid with narrow pleats, my favorite, though it didn't fit well. I liked the forest green of the fabric, its fine woolen weave, and the subtle blue, black, and red threads that created the plaid. I wore this skirt with a white blouse and yellow sweater, and I imagined it made me look like the rich white girls who lived in Park Hills.

To wear green on a Thursday meant running the risk of being taunted, should anyone remember this ancient rule and decide to employ it against some forgetful soul. To avoid these taunts, my best friend and I segregated ourselves from the popular kids. We sought the protective staircase where we could discuss our daydreams about other girls without fear of intrusion. Sometimes we plotted our strategy as "pirates" for the next time we went sailing in her family's small sailboat. In Mariner Scouts we learned to flag one another in semaphore, the sailor's code, which we cleverly converted into a writing system to send notes back and forth in our classes.

My friend and I took as many classes together as we could, but inevitably one of us would be left alone in some humiliating circumstance. For me, that proved to be the sewing class that fulfilled the "Home Ec" requirement. Every girl was obliged to take this class, to learn how to be a good home-maker for her future husband and family. Even my older sister complained about this course. Why do the boys get to take fun classes like Shop, she would ask, and learn how to use tools and build things? I also thought it was unfair not to be given the opportunity to learn how to use a saw or screw-driver, to make a lamp or an archery bow. I imagined myself building a doghouse, and then making a little mailbox for it, and a sign on a post pointing the direction to Toto's door. But no, I would have to make an A-line skirt in Mrs. McMahon's class, the crabbiest teacher on campus. I would have to learn to use pinking shears and mark fabric with blue chalk. I would have to guide my skirt beneath the terrifying needle, my knee controlling the speed of the stitch. I would have to make a skirt that I would be proud and happy to wear. The success of my skirt would demonstrate that I was a real girl with an interest in being female and eventually a wife and mother. It would prove a love for my body, a vanity in my looks, a desire to be desired by boys.

Oh, the hours I wasted in Mrs. McMahon's class! For days I attempted to thread my machine. For weeks I contemplated the bobbin. For a whole quarter I tried unsuccessfully to lay out my skirt according to the mysteries of the woven fabric. Thank God for the flu that wiped me out for three weeks. And when I returned to school, I managed to break my little finger playing softball. The aluminum cast and Ace bandage on my left hand increased my clumsiness so much I didn't even have to pretend.

One day I knew I'd have to put the pieces of the skirt to-gether, hem it, sew on the waistband and then do the hardest thing of all, the buttonhole and button. At home, Mama usu-ally sewed our clothes. There she'd be in the afternoon, the machine set up at one end of the dining room table, with pat-terns, pins, and scraps of fabric everywhere. The only thing my mother hated to sew was buttonholes. This she asked my father to do. So after dinner, perhaps on a Thursday evening, my father would hoist the Pfaff back up on the table and sit down to sew. A symphony would pour from the FM station he had dialed on the radio in its wooden cabinet. Dad would put his knees primly together, and his face would register satisfaction. He would thread the machine, take the skirt or blouse or whatever Mom had stitched together, and gently touching the pedal with his foot, guide the needle into creating a buttonhole that my mom would later slit open with a razor blade. "Don't ever tell your friends your father knows how to sew," Mom would say. "People will laugh. They won't understand. They'll say he must be a queer!"

A Berkeley Life

1.
Most of my life I looked out
over the bay, over the blue
water and bridge
to the white city that gleamed
in the morning sun.
Beyond the white city was the ocean
curving into an infinity of birds
and waves. Somewhere
at the far end of the imagination
lay Japan, from whose fishing fleet
drifted the glass floats
we sometimes found
among dry strands of seaweed
on excursions to the beach.

The hills were a place of mud and rain,
of pungent chaparral, of oak,
laurel, and thistle. Past the narrow
asphalt streets and the gray-leaved eucalyptus,
we took our dogs into the hills
on foggy mornings, or cloudless
winter evenings, when my father
returned tired from work
and his long commute.
We watched as Berkeley changed—
the university expanded, the city
widened streets or blocked off others,
the traffic became busier.

And on those evenings, one year
or another as I got older,
a girl and I would sometimes
walk out to the steep green hills
above the labs and think tanks,
above the groves, the stadium,
the student housing.

Lit from underneath, the fog
glared over the city.
The sound of traffic rose to our ears,
a continuous throb. Then,
not looking at her face,
I would put my arm
around her shoulder.
If she did not move away—
if she leaned her head toward me—
we would stand thus, together,
in a world that did not see us.

2.
Flowering trees, wind,
the south slope of sun,
a Mediterranean pine,
blossoming yucca.
The night smell
of star jasmine.
This was my neighborhood:
streets clean, almost
suburban.
Inside people's houses
I imagined bookcases,
a piano, the sideboard
with its carafe of rich liquor,
matching glasses.
Warm light. Adults
in conversation, children asleep
in cartoon-patterned pajamas.

The men are lawyers,
accountants, university professors.
They live
a good life:
opera, theater,
foreign films,
art openings, things
I cannot imagine.
They drive Volvos,
Peugeots, the occasional
Mercedes. And their wives
dress in linen
or chic satin
evening clothes.
I babysit their children
in homes that are always clean.
(The cleaning lady
comes on Friday.)

I look out the large windows
of their new houses.
The wooden frames smell fresh,
the glass is unbuckled.
Outside, the sky is very dark,
so dark you can see stars
though the lights below twinkle.

Shoes still on,
I fall asleep
on their cream-colored sofa.
They come home quietly,
their voices low, clothes
rustling. They pay cash.
The husband drives me home,
while the wife who is
so beautiful, so pale,
removes her clothes,
her makeup. She
waits for him
to return.

He drops me off at
the curb of my house
with its tangled
vegetation, old trees,
steep stairs.
I enter the hall
with its dog smell,
musty dampness,
the smell of disorder
and family secrets.

3.
"Dennis, goddamit,
come back here!"
That was my older sister
hollering from the porch
at her boyfriend
whom my mother,
in a fit of compassion,
had invited to live with us.
The motor of the '49 Ford
Mom gave him
roars as Dennis
peels away.
My sister cries,
slams doors,
tells our mother to
shut up!
Dennis will call later that evening,
drunk, but sobered from fear:
he has slammed the car into a telephone pole
by the canyon bar, a bar for misfit
cowboys in the Oakland hills.

He will come home reeking of liquor
and stumble into the room
where my younger sister and I sleep.
Trying to kiss her,
slobbering,
he stinks of beer,
cigarettes, shaving lotion.
He paws her with his rough
strong hands.
"Get away," shrieks my younger sister.
"Quit bothering me!"

Dennis will be crying, unsteady,
stupid. In the morning
Mother will be mad at him.
But as if he's her son,
or the man in the family,
she will pick up
his jeans and shorts,
cook his breakfast,
do his laundry—
laundry I fold, iron,
and place on the bed
in his room.
He flatters my mother
with his dog-like appreciation.
She believes in his innocence,
and berates my older sister.
"You're no better than a whore,
you chippy. You'll never
amount to anything!"
My dad, meanwhile, says nothing.
He gets up each morning
and drives away.

Our older sister is bad-tempered,
angry.
She hates us.
We keep away from her.
Every day
she screams,
slams doors.
She can never say
what happened.

Every day
the structure of our Berkeley life
promises to give way.

Easter Sunday

Easter Sunday and my father plans a visit to one of the old missions along the Camino Real. After church we get on the highway and begin our journey. It is late March or early April. The sky is azure and clouds scud in from the Pacific, thick and white. They break apart as they pass over the coast range, and the broken fragments, still large, move swiftly over the land. The land is green, not the green of Germany as I have heard it reported, but a green full of sunlight and rapid change. If the winter and spring rains have been sufficient, the presence of last year's grasses will be hidden, their gray stalks covered by fresh growth. This spring the sturdy flowers have opened, and my mother reels off the endless list of names as we pass them by: lupine, California poppy, clarkia, larkspur, Indian paintbrush, owl's clover, buttercup, vetch, trillium, forget-me-not, columbine, fairy's lantern, pearly everlasting. The species are so mixed we hardly know the indigenous from the introduced, the native from the volunteer, the survivor from the parasite populations that have sprung up in the friendly habitat. This is California with its rich, false history. Whatever direction one goes, north or south, the flowers mark boundaries, the possibility of their appearance determined by many things: hills or gullies, rainfall or drought, ranches or subdivisions, the presence of other like-minded plants and trees.

We drive far south to the mission in the Los Padres Mountains. Here, at the far end of a long, fertile valley, the military has established a base. It is difficult to understand the need for weapons or to feel cheered by the hard-faced, uniformed men, armored vehicles, and what appear to be the underground houses for missiles. No one wants to talk about the war, which explodes somewhere else with wearisome regularity each night on television. It is Sunday, Easter; the family is enjoying a rare peace. The day is beautiful and the hills sacred. It is hard to imagine destruction. At the mission, the enclosed courtyard is dry and warm, bees buzz among the cactus and purple roses. In the small adobe cells, opened for our inspection, are the accoutrements of the Franciscans, solemn crucifixes nailed above their skinny beds. In other rooms the Indians worked, tanning leather, shoeing horses, cooking the padres' soup. In these troughs, the Indians were fed. Beyond the mission are the remnants of *hornos* and corrals, the fields of wild bulbs and clover the Indians longed to eat. Under one portico, a shiver moves up my spine: the dead, I know suddenly, are buried in the walls, among the arches, and beneath this well-tamped earth.

Across the mountains, not far as the raven flies, lies the ocean, the jagged edge of the continent.

My Father

I have tried to understand
what makes me afraid, wondering
what my sisters and I will do
with the body of my father
when he dies.
While in his seventies
he changed his sex,
becoming a woman
like us.

As a man, my father was not beautiful.
The skin on his chest was fish white,
he was ruddy at the neck,
his muscles were stringy.
The veins showed on the backs of his hands.
Standing, he gave no pose of strength,
nothing stern, nothing possessive.
He never wished to take up space.
Of the two, my mother was the angrier:
her curses brought my father to shame.
I remember his response to her,
the set line of his mouth,
his lips pressed firmly together.

As a woman, is my father beautiful?
Sometimes in the morning
he calls me long distance.
His voice is softer.
I know it's the voice he uses as Cynthia.
He asks how I am.
I want to say, "I am trying
to deal with my fear of you.
If it weren't for that,
I'd be fine."

In the letters he wrote me
after my mother died,
he said, "When you last came home,
I'm sure you noticed
I've changed. I have been taking hormones
these last few years.
It must be no surprise."

He wrote, "Now that I am a woman
I like to go dancing.
One night Eduardo walked me to my car.
As we stood there, Eduardo wanted to hug me.
I allowed him to put his arms around me.
Suddenly he was feeling me up,
his hands on my breasts.
It was a strange sensation.
I liked it very much.
I don't know if I want to see him again."

Those letters!
I threw them on the floor.
I wanted to stomp on them.
"Your mother," he wrote,
"got the notion when you were young
that you were not normal.
Perhaps it was because
you hated to wear dresses.
She took you to the pediatrician one day,
remarking that if he found anything wrong with you
she would kill you,
then kill herself. Of course,
after the doctor poked and prodded,
he declared there was absolutely
nothing wrong with you."

"Your mother," he wrote again,
"was no saint. Your cousin Elaine
was not your cousin at all
but a half sister by an Indian father,
your mother's lover.
I agreed to raise her as my daughter,
but your mother was so hard on the poor girl
she ran away. Your mother would never
acknowledge her as her own."

"Don't tell your sisters any of this,"
he begged. "It must remain a secret."

O, my father,
father I never knew,
father who never was
yet was my only father,
who do you imagine I am?

Would my father remember the time
I tried to run away from home?
Up as early as him,
my suitcase already packed
and placed on the dark front porch,
I caught the first bus downtown.
He never even knew that I left.
Later he found me at the Greyhound station,
bus ticket in hand.
"Let's go home," he said.
"She hates me," I said.
"I know," he replied.

Then I wept.
I wanted him to hug me,
but he stood, embarrassed,
his arms at his sides.
"Please," he whispered,
"don't make a scene in public."

What will my sisters and I do
on the day of your death?
Where will you be?
At home,
or in the apartment you rented
in that city we do not know?
Will someone be with you?
You have always been so alone.
Will your death come in the fall
or the spring?
Will it be when the hills
have turned green in California?
Will the pear orchards be in blossom?
Will you die on the interstate
near a fallow field
where blackbirds have settled
because it is evening?

But I don't want to think about it.
Whom will we tell?
What will we tell them?

"No one will be able to tell the difference,"
my father wrote. "I will be anatomically perfect."

Our House

Our house knows too much
and that is why our father let it fall
into ruin, beneath the weight of mother's cancer
and his own lapses of memory.

Only the most tender could live there now,
running her hand along the walls,
touching the things we all touched:
the warped panels of a cedar closet,
the yellowed keys of the piano.

Only the strongest could begin repairs,
shoring up the old foundation,
or ascend to the top of the house and remove,
one by one, the heavy tiles,
rip back tar and paper.

Only the fiercest could know what our house knows,
could open doors and windows, release
the strange voices that inhabit deserted bedrooms.

A Journey

On the eve of the day people set their clocks forward, two
young women, sisters, travel north on a commercial bus line.
The day is rainy and cold, the long pastures in the Central Val-
ley dark and muddy, and the new crops of wheat and alfalfa
are just beginning to top the soil. Winter is barely over; even
with the extra hour of daylight, evening will come early.
Though it seems old-fashioned, and neither will admit it, the
sisters travel together for protection as much as for one an-
other's company. The younger of the two has just turned
twenty-one, and this is her first adventure as a true adult who
is not obliged to report her life to her parents. Her sister, older
by a year and a half, and married, carries with her the gravity
of being the firstborn. They are going together to work on a
ranch far out along the banks of one of the great western
rivers.

The journey lasts all night, and late the next day they are
watching the river whose headwaters form, gather, and rush
down out of mountains in Canada. The wet shale cliffs and
forested hills are intensely beautiful, and the younger sister
wishes they could travel another night, and another, far into
the heartland of the country. She feels a little scared at the
idea of meeting her new employers. All day she has sup-
pressed a certain kind of loneliness at leaving her mother, a
homesickness she can scarcely acknowledge. It makes her
thankful for her sister's company.

When their mother is about to die, years later, these two will
flank her body, the older gently holding the old woman up-
right, the younger coaxing their mother's spirit out. "Follow
the light, mama, follow the light." Like watching a peculiar
birth—the labored breathing, the weariness—the two stand
on the brink of a long awakening: it is now their job to gather

into themselves bereftness, love, and all that remains hard and inarticulate. They take the world, like a full basket, onto their shoulders. Their mother's brow is covered with dampness, and their brows sweat too, as they work quietly and with concentration to help their mother leave.

Mama's Girl

Some days I wish I could go home.
I sit on the sofa and think about my mother,
gone nine years. It doesn't seem so long.
I can see her face, brown as a walnut,
her fierce black eyes, and strong hair
turned silver from chemotherapy.

In spite of years away, I always returned,
a regular mama's girl, needing
to sit with my mom of an evening.
"When I go," she'd say, "I want you
to find someone to love,
someone steady."

Having accepted, finally,
my attraction to women, mama would add,
"She should be mature,
and able to love you completely.
Not like those who take your heart,
throw it on the ground,
and trample it like dirt."

I'd think of girls I'd known,
women who tried to love me,
or make me love them.
It was odd how consistently
I'd choose the most impossible:
someone married, someone religious,
someone crazy.
Someone who never gave a blue fuck
what happened to me when she
picked up with a man, nuzzled him
in front of me, and laughed
at my discomfort and pain.
"You can't handle it," she'd say.
"I want to be a free spirit."

Well yes, that's true. All those years
I'd go home and try
to find another thing to do:
a job, more school, or sit at my desk
and write, alone in my room.

Outside the fog blew through the redwood trees,
while down the hall mom would be holding back
whatever frightened her most about our lives.

Burdens of the Heart

Companion

I chose a woman who would not deny
the burning core of me.
She embraces fire so tenderly
my heart changes to a salmon and leaps
into her net of moist hair.

I chose a woman who would not resist
the ebb and crest of my longing.
She watches the ocean so lovingly
the waves become birds
who fly to a ripening tree.

I chose a woman who would not violate
the sacred trust of my body.
She regards me so steadily
my heart becomes a bell
clanging wildly in the wind.

I chose a woman who would not silence
the words of her own desire.
She closes distances so exactly
my heart changes into a star
falling through the night sky.

I chose a woman who would not refuse
to mother my infancy.
Between her legs all things are born.
At her breast everything has life.

She cradles my heart so soundly,
it gleams like a ruby, burnished
and bright in her hand.

When I Lived by the River

"Fucking queer," he said.
"I ought to beat the shit out of you.
Your kind would be better off dead!"
We were driving around the back woods
in the state of Washington
at night.
It was winter.
The cold stars
shone in the dense sky,
so many stars
in their strange unearthly hues:
purple, magenta, some
the color of honey,
some like blood-red lava.
The snow lay on the meadows,
tranquil pastures
bordered by willows
and dark Douglas fir.

In the car were six of us,
maybe seven,
and a case of beer
half drunk.
I was twenty-one,
the one who delivered
that cold frothy liquid,
placing it in the back seat of the car.

"You almost killed that one guy," said Jeanie.
She was my co-worker.
"They found him in a ditch
with his ribs crushed
and his face shoved in."
"Yeah," replied Tom,
"and that's why I can't
cross the state line,
that's why me and Billy
are hiding out
on this side of the river.
Ain't that right, Billy?"
Billy mumbled, gave a sleepy nod.

The river looked ominous,
huge and wide, that green water
full of suckholes so large
they could swallow a car
if you were unlucky enough
to skid off the road
on the black ice.
You'd plunge
through the guardrails,
the willows, the patterns of ice
that had formed on the chilly
lip of the river.

I wondered if the boys were lying.
Not six hours before
all of us had gone to a tavern
on the south end of town—
we were in Oregon, across the river—
and shared at least
two pitchers.
It was after work,
after the long shift
in the fishing-lure factory
where all that snowy afternoon
we women assembled
Li'l Chief Smokers.

At work it was me, Jeanie,
Dee, and the others:
the old woman who smelled bad,
the mother-daughter teams,
the sexy redhead,
the quiet little blonde
with the pink parka.
And of course there were Okies—
that's what the redhead called them—
a girl who lived in a Quonset hut
in the muddy apple orchard,
a woman who lived at the south end
of the green Hood River valley.
One day she'd said to me,
"Aren't you an Indian?
You look like my relatives
in Oklahoma.
Just like," she said.
And she mused on my features
till I got embarrassed.
She was pretty, a loner.
I was afraid
I'd fall for her.

Earlier, at the tavern,
I was squeezed behind the table
with Jeanie on one side
and a wall on the other.
And Tom, or Billy,
or whoever,
was already bleary-eyed,
muttering to himself,
viciously berating Jeanie
in a monotonous chant:
"cunt, cunt, cunt, cunt!"
"Stop that!" said Jeanie.
"Don't call me that."
"You shit," she said.
"Who do you think you are?"
He just kept chanting,
his lips turned down
like a fish's mouth.

"Don't worry," said Jeanie—
this was much later—
"he won't beat you.
He's too drunk."
I remember they had made love,
her and Tom,
in her apartment.
We'd gone there after the tavern
to continue our drinking.
I was dozing in front of the TV
when I was awakened
by Tom's fierce grunts
and Jeanie moaning, writhing so hard
her wig popped off her head.
A wig! I was surprised. I thought
I'd never seen anything
less romantic.

Again in the car
somewhere back of the river,
on a ridge above the woods
and frozen meadows,
we turned towards town,
headed back towards the river.
"I will too beat her up,"
said Tom, "soon as I find a place
to pull over.
I'll beat the shit
out of her,
fucking little queer,
thinks she's some kind of man!"

"Just let him talk," whispered Jeanie.
"Don't answer.
It's all just talk."

And pretty soon he shut up.
For a time we were silent
driving through the wild
lonely night
with snow all around,
the stars gleaming like amber.
I wanted to go home,
back to my solitary existence.

Finally on the highway,
near the lane to my trailer,
Tom stopped the car, and,
almost courteously,
let me out by the side of the road.
Then off they sped,
without a word.

I stood for a moment,
wavering. A mist
had formed along the river,
had rolled up over the highway,
the pastures.
I wanted to walk into it,
to walk forever.
I wanted to disappear.

Snow

Snow had fallen during the night,
snow on snow. The streets were white and muffled,
and hard banks had piled up along the sidewalks,
on the boulevard where city buses chuffed to a stop.
It seemed we disembarked into caves of ice,
into dirty passages broken through by passersby
heading for home after the five o'clock
rush from downtown.

I liked the snow, the way the city slowed
to accommodate Nature
who slid her hand over the Northwest,
from Puget Sound
to the Willamette Valley,
from Tillamook to Hood River,
until fields, forests,
the rounded hills and orchards
all lay in a deep frosty dream:
ponds frozen over,
cattails split like cornhusks,
horses in pastures,
breath steaming, icicles
hanging from their shaggy coats.

The morning after the snow
it was just growing light.
And probably for the first time
I saw two adults in love.
He had walked out from their basement apartment,
laughing as he pushed through
that trench of cold powder,
a stocky black man
in a bus driver's uniform.
She was at the door, laughing with him,
her blonde hair disheveled,
her face puffy.
She smoked a cigarette, he held
a cup of coffee.
Before quite reaching the street
he had come back to kiss her.

That is what I saw
as I watched from my window:
him waving to her from the corner
as he strode through the snow,
the fresh swirl blown down like feathers
or cottony seeds.

That winter, for me,
was a time of transition.
Yet everything seemed to fit together:
how you and I read César Vallejo,
drank strong French coffee,
and ate chunks of bittersweet chocolate.
How the soft sounds of Portuguese
fit in my mouth
as we studied from one of your books.
How every day, downtown, we passed
the blind man who played the accordion,
and the family of women who stood
in a storefront window
at the foot of Ankeny Bridge—
women young and old,
their faces hardened,
black hair pulled tight
against their thin heads.
I believed they were gypsies
who could see into my soul.

They would have seen how I
was in love with you,
a girl who was a little crazy,
who had hung her heart
in the icy branches of a tree
beyond the reach of
father, mother, or lover.
How stupidly I behaved with you.
But I was young, frightened,
and also crazy.
I didn't know the dimensions
of abuse and violence;
I was still unnerved
by the word "lesbian,"
how it began with a shameful lateral,
how the sibilance of its interior
fit against the body with its wetness,
its caverns,
its long dream of winter.

Perhaps that's why I like
to think of the busman and his woman,
the warmth that flooded out their door
as if they'd stepped from their hot sheets
to the shower, to the breakfast table
with its cups of coffee,
how their flesh was still flushed
with blood and kisses.
                          I know this now,
the depth of roses, the laughter
that resounds in frozen air,
the first shove through January snowfall.
After years I grew up,
married a woman who isn't crazy.
I like to imagine how
I've come back to kiss her,
time after time on snowy mornings,
her lips warm,
the room steaming,
the smell of sex still in our bed
delicious as sweet rolls and tangerines.

I Learn a Lesson about Our Society

Late November on our way to work
you pulled the cord and the bus stopped
this side of the Alameda tube.
"I've got to get out of here,"
you told me abruptly.
"Please, don't follow me."
I looked in your face
but you wouldn't look back.
You were nervous,
your eyes moving everywhere.
"I'll phone," you said.
I watched you push your way
through the press of students,
secretaries, the eight a.m.
crowd on their way to work.
Eyes glazed, you stepped off the bus.

I didn't know then it was epilepsy
that jerked you to your feet,
and like a pistol against the skull,
compelled you to walk,
walk, making your way to 14th Avenue,
your jaw clamped as if it had been wired closed.
You knew places where you could abort the attack
with heroin: back porches
where men of every color shot up,
a hard gang of hard-asses, and you,
skinny and tough as the boy
you wished you could be.

Those were times of no time for you,
weeklong blackouts in which you lost
all trace of your history,
name, or family.
Your kids would be alone in the house,
eating cold hot dogs and white bread.
They were used to taking care of themselves.

After an attack, you woke here or there
and had to find your way home.
Sometimes you came to on the stone
cold floor of a cell.
Other times, like that day,
you ended up in the hospital
on some ward in the basement,
strapped down on a table.
The nurses and orderlies abused you,
kept the restraints on you for hours.
They despised you for being an addict,
a queer, at the mercy
of an illness.

It was then I learned things
I never knew before: that privilege
is a form of ignorance,
that the poor are the enemy of the state.
And not the poor alone, but the sick,
criminal, crazy, queer, young,
old, and disabled.
No matter what color we are,
no matter what language we speak.
Every person, I suppose, must come
to this understanding: it's not your right
to question the police, the army,
any number of authorities.
If you pass, sucker,
it's because they let you pass.

And I have you to thank for this, my friend,
though in the end we broke up like any couple
where jealousy is involved.
I, who thought I was so butch,
got tired of playing mistress
to your drugs. You were married
to a poison you loved
almost better than life itself.

It happened three weeks later,
Christmas nearly upon us,
fake ice in the windows, fake snow,
and the yellow glare of lights
around the lots of cut trees.
The usual cold fog
had rolled down from Sacramento.
Out on the Nimitz freeway
you began to pound my arm.
"Oh please, goddamn it,
please," you kept saying.
Then you cracked the windshield
with your fist, and I took
the next exit, obedient,
while you directed me to the house
on that particular dirty street.
I waited in the car watching the children,
the drunks, listening to sirens,
jet noise, the freeway.

When you came out you were happy,
calm as a butterfly
who had closed her wings.

Amorcita

My love,
who this afternoon
awaited my arrival,
who turned to me
as I opened my arms,
who kissed me
while I strummed my guitar—
you stand by the window
where rain is falling
and look out on the busy street.

Sixteen, skinny,
two years married,
living here in the far north,
you smoke cigarettes,
one after the other,
and speak in a husky voice.

You tell me of earthquakes,
and Somoza's army,
of drought, and mysterious
occult forces.
You tell me about the serpent
who loved you, and how
your father killed it
with a machete.

You speak, too, of the steamy
volcanos, of holes in the earth
that gape suddenly open,
and of the man
who married your sister—
how he tied her wrists
to the head of their bed,
then stubbed out his cigars
on her elegant legs.

You remember the *duendes*
and slow-moving iguanas;
the blond North Americans
at the head of military columns;
and nuns at the Catholic school
who bathed you in a galvanized washtub
without removing your petticoat.

Sometimes, too, you speak of the river
which, after the rain, carried animals
and humans: a hand, a flayed head,
the carcass of a horse.

You miss the smell of cornfields
and the burned taste of coffee,
the black beans of home,
the chiles from your region.
You want to dance again
to your country's strong rhythms,
and hear the voice of your aging father.

My friend, my girl,
my amorcita,
I see you by the window
where rain keeps falling,
tapping your foot on the floor.
I wish that I could make you happy.

"Mi pobre país," I hear you whisper.
"Poor little Nicaragua!"

Earthquake Weather

It's earthquake weather in California,
that hazy stillness along the coast
just before the Santa Anas howl
out of the east, hot and dry.

There were days in September when we drove
down the fault line south of Hayward.
We went where there were Spanish names:
Suñol and Calaveras,
la Misión de San José.
I remember seeing the cells of the padres,
their faded vestments,
the implements of wood and iron.

We were looking for another country,
something not North America:
a taste, a smell, a solitary image—
the eucalyptus on a bleached hill.
Its blue pungent leaves made you long
for another home.

That was what you wanted from me—
to be your other home,
your other country.
Being Indian, I was your *cholo*
from the Bolivian highlands.
I was your boy, full of stone
and a cold sunset.

At night, seated at your bedside,
I was remote. I often made you weep—
you in the guise of an *angelita*.
You lay on the low mattress,
a weaving beneath your head,
and watched me with your slow eyes,
your sadness.

When September comes with its hot,
electric winds,
I will think of you and know
somewhere in the world
the earth is breaking open.

Your Least Good Lover

One day you were in the little café where I worked.
I was upstairs slicing meat, while downstairs
you ordered a coffee with your friends.
I could see you from the loft where I stood.

How long had it been? Three years?
I went off my shift,
came downstairs,
and walked to your table.
You acted as if it were perfectly natural
and introduced me to the women you were with.
Then we sat together, talking.
You looked happy to see me.
Happy, but wary.

That was the beginning of the last
stage of our friendship.
It was fall time, I remember,
and you invited me to Fresno.
I drove down 99 East
to sleep in your bed
beneath a poster of Gauguin's
native women.
I remember your dead-end
street by the county airport,
the house on its sandy foundation,
sycamores in the dry yard,
spiny cactus.

You made it clear to me: I was your least
good lover. But how I loved you!
The curve of your white girl's hip,
your rib cage of delicate bones,
the pale color of your breasts,
the way your eyelids fluttered like small moths
as you tipped your head back,
chin toward the ceiling.
I loved looking at your naked legs
as you got up from the bed
and walked across the floor for a book,
a poem.

Do you remember how the rain fell
that October? Hard
and beautiful.
I was driving in rain, in fog,
through the orchards,
past yards of marigolds
yellow as flames.
It rained in the foothills
where the Miwok still live.

Too bad about your passion,
your other lovers. Too bad for me.
Once you told me about an Indian
boy who had a crush on you.
Your first boyfriend.
He would tease you, you said,
by pulling down the zipper
on a favorite sweater you wore.

Sometimes I envied that boy.
Other times I felt pity.
I could see the exact look in his face
when he gazed at you. His dark eyes.
His dark hair. He must have trembled,
hating you and wanting you.

You must have trembled too,
waiting for his mocking aggression.
I know how scared you can be,
and how cold. How pained you've felt,
but also, how free.

On Point Reyes

In midsummer we hiked in a range of hills
above Point Reyes: you, me,
your man, and some companions.
In the meadows the grass was green and high;
poison oak grew in lush thickets,
and in the cool soil of creekbeds
nettles pricked our legs.

I remember the previous summer,
how I took you to a river farther north:
past the vineyards, the lava country,
the defunct lumber mills of Mendocino County.
In that backcountry of oaks and pines
we followed a narrow canyon.
The day was hot and cloudless.
At a wide spot in the road we stopped,
scrambled down a steep bank.
Then for a long time we sat
on the sandy river's edge, talking,
before we took off our clothes
and plunged in.

Later, sitting side by side in the afternoon sun,
you stroked my leg and told me
I looked strong.
Earlier, I had watched you backfloat
in the shimmering river. Your breasts rose
like curved petals in the verdant water,
and your hair streamed like an aureole
around your face.

Writing now of these times I imagine
your objections: how I am making of our friendship
a public record, that something is faulty
in the reconstruction, that this writing
constitutes an act of betrayal.
Yet would you deny
that between women desire exists,
that in our friendship a delicate
and erotic strand of fire unites us?
Because I remember moments
when we waited, not only to be alone,
but for something else:
how you would allow me to embrace you,
or almost trembling, you would stroke my leg.

On the coast above Point Reyes we found such a moment.
The others had walked ahead
and we were among trees—
spruce and alder.
A breeze from the ocean had picked up
and a bank of fog was forming
out at the Farralones.
We did not have much time
before we caught up with the others
who waited for us at the roadhead.

I can still see how you looked at me—
tender, open, unafraid.
Then I asked, "Do you remember
the time at the river?"
When you answered, "I'll never forget,"
the day flooded back for me
with its heat and sunlight,
the green of the river,
the way you dove and glided
beneath its surface—
like an ouzel, an otter—
while the parched grass wavered
on the steep coastal hills.

A Flirtation

When you stroked my cheek in public
as if I were a boy,
and asked had I shaved this week,
we both laughed.
You are such a flirt!

I've watched with admiration
the way you enter a room,
the way you leave.
I like the way you hold
my attention with your eyes.
I'm no stone!
For days I remembered how your fingers
lingered on my face,
their brief pressure against my skin,
and the flush that spread up my throat,
across my chin.

Earlier, in the hotel lobby,
you sat in a chair,
and I reclined at your feet.
We were alone
except for the wedding party in the next room,
the occasional late guest
who arrived in evening clothes.

You leaned forward
watching me, intense.
I thought you were going to ask me
for a kiss.
If I weren't already married and in love,
I could pretend we might have rolled
on the plush carpet like groom and bride.

You would have let me ride, little pony,
ride into those Oklahoma hills.

Late Summer in the Sierra

1.
Our friend shows me snapshots:
late summer in the Sierra,
the river full of light,
rocks and sand the color of gold.
On the opposite shore, sugar pines
sway in the hot afternoon breeze.
You stand in the water calf-deep,
naked, partly facing the camera.
You are modest and a little shy.
I can see the exact shape of your breasts
and smooth belly.
You are smiling,
bending slightly towards the water.

2.
In another photo you are squatting
with the baby in your arms.
You are still by the river,
and the baby lies across your lap.
She looks to be squirming, cranky.
You look toward the photographer
whose shadow leans across you.
Though you are laughing,
the camera seems a little invasive.
But the one who takes the pictures teases you,
and everyone is in a good humor, except the baby
who fusses before falling asleep.

3.
In late afternoon you pack to go home.
Everyone is quiet, the child
slumbering in our friend's arms.
You can hear the sound of water above the swimming hole
where the river curves around a rock.
It is less hot, cool in the shadow of trees.
All day blackberries have ripened.
You pick them as you walk along,
pausing in the shade,
eating berries off the vine.
Some are sweet, some tart.
The juice is very red.
They leave a stain on your fingers,
a suggestion of invisible thorns.

4.
Our friend with the snapshots leaves the room
and I am alone with these images—
your clear eyes and brow,
the laughing mouth I have watched,
sometimes tight with anguish.
Your skin with its fine, soft weave.

The burdens of the heart are these:
a declaration of love that remains inert,
a kiss that stays unbidden.
The passion of the body—
suspended—
till it can circulate through the soul
like cold pure water.

Days Without You

Days without you I collect myself around my work, writing, reading old philosophers who make nonsense out of everything. All I want to do is gaze out the window at the cottonwoods across the way. Their green leaves shimmer in the morning heat, and the whir of cicadas begins like the sound of the hunchback's wild flute that travels out of Indian time on the immemorial wind. A cluster of blue clouds has formed behind the mountains.

When I drive out to the airport to meet you, I feel a little crazy. Everywhere the graffiti of murderous boys is scrawled on bullet-punctuated walls. Neighborhoods crumble beneath signs for liquor, real estate, and cigarettes. Then the squared lines of the airport rise up, and I enter the antiseptic world of new buildings. The floors have been polished, the pastel tiles glow. I wait for you this rainy August evening, nervous and alert. When you disembark from the plane, you are smiling and pretty, but as always, we pretend to be just friends and walk out together, barely touching. It is only in the underground parking where no one can see our passion that you suddenly lean over to me and open your mouth against mine. Then there is such a rush that my heart lunges, and I'm shy and in love with you, woman who shares my life.

Later, driving up Central, you put your hand on my thigh and the same thing happens. "Life is good," you say. "Don't you wish we were rich?" But we are. We're rich and foreign as the dinner we just ate off hot solid plates: edged with the piquancy of sauce and hard tears of garlic, graced with basil and thyme to a perfect measure, fresh as the pale butter, crusty loaf, and earthy wine.

About the Author

Janice Gould is a mixedblood European/Koyangk'auwi Maidu who grew up in Berkeley, California. She earned a B.A. in linguistics and an M.A. in English from the University of California, Berkeley, and is now working toward a Ph.D. in English at the University of New Mexico. She was recently awarded a Ford Fellowship for her dissertation work on American Indian women's poetry. Gould's poetry has also been recognized with grants from the National Endowment for the Arts and the Astraea Foundation.

Gould's first poem was published in 1971, and her work appeared in feminist journals and anthologies throughout the 1980s. Her first collection of poetry, *Beneath My Heart*, was published in 1990.

In addition to being a student and writer, Gould has taught courses in American Indian literature at the College of Santa Fe in Albuquerque and courses in American studies, creative writing, and women's studies at the University of New Mexico. In 1994 and 1995, she was invited to teach a poetry workshop at a woman's writing retreat called "Flight of the Mind," outside Eugene, Oregon. She has also taught a poetry workshop to teens through a program called "Celebrate Youth" housed at the College of Santa Fe.

Gould now lives in Albuquerque with her partner of several years and their numerous cats.